How to Buy 1000 Bricks

A Step-By-Step Guide to Buying Real Estate

Bud Streten

Table of Contents

Chapter 1 About The Author 1

Chapter 2 What is your strategy? 4

    Strong capital gains 4

    High Rental Yield 5

    Renovate 5

    Example 1. Gold Coast, Queensland Australia (Buy and Sell) 6

    Example 2 Bellmere, Queensland Australia (Buy and hold) . 6

Chapter 3 Build Your Team 8

    Buyer's Agent 8

    Strategy 10

    Legal 10

    Finance 11

    The Search 11

    Inspection 12

    Negotiations 13

    Contract conditions 13

    Lending Manager 13

- Conveyancer 14
- What is a conveyancer? 14
- Financial Advisor 15
- Bullets from Bud 16

Chapter 4 Finance 17

- What is a mortgage? 19
- Bill Gates famously once said, "With great wealth comes great responsibility." 20
- Bullets from Bud 21
- Essential Pre-Purchasing Costs To Account For 21
- Essential fees to consider when building your budget. 22
- Bullets from Bud 24
- Lenders Mortgage Insurance (LMI) 24
- Interest Rates 25
- How is interest calculated on a home loan? 25
- What affects interest rates? 26
- How to reduce the amount of interest paid? 27
- Pre-Approval 28
- Pre-approvals expire, ... 29
- If the property is unacceptable, will my loan not be approved? 30
- You may not be approved if your circumstances change. ... 30
- Changes to interest rates can affect your pre-approval. ... 31
- Pre-approval tells sellers that you're serious about buying. . 31

Chapter 5 Define Your Area 33

Budget 34

Desirability 34

Work..36

School..36

Growth..37

Large infrastructure projects: 40

Chapter 6 Define Your Property 41

House: 42

Terraces: 43

Semi-Detached House: 43

Duplex: 44

Townhouse: 45

Apartments: 46

Chapter 7 Starting Your Search 48

Parameters: 48

Alerts: 50

Keeping track: 50

Chapter 8 Shortlisting Your Search 52

Chapter 9 Inspecting the Property..56

Take in the home as a whole 56

Don't be shy check all the nooks and crannies. 57

Remember the things you can't see 57

Chapter 10 Making an Offer 59

Chapter 11 Contract of Sale 64

Chapter 12 Finance Conditions 66

What is a finance clause in a contract of sale? 66

How does a finance clause work? 66

Requesting an extension 67

Involve the bank 68

Reviewing your finance offer 69

Advise your conveyancer 69

Signing and returning the loan documents 69

Chapter 13 Building and Pest Conditions 71

Conditions, from the date of the contract: 71

What happens on the day of the Building and Pest Inspection? 72

Chapter 14 Other Conditions 75

Chapter 15 Unconditional Contract 77

What is an unconditional contract 77

Property condition: 78

Finance 79

Evaluation 79

What now that your contract is unconditional? 79

Organising utilities 79

Six weeks out - Decide what you want to take with you and clean 80

Five weeks out - Sell or discard your unwanted items 81

Four weeks out - Organise how to move your home 81

Two weeks out - Start packing! 82

    One week to go - The final countdown 82

Chapter 16 Pre-settlement Inspection 84

    What should you be looking for? 85

    Significant damage 85

    Inclusions and exclusions 85

    Condition 86

    Special conditions 86

Chapter 17 Settlement Day 87

Chapter 1
About The Author

Bud was born in Katherine, Northern Territory, in 1986. His parents divorced when he was three, and he always lived in rented homes. Bud's Mum moved them to his uncle and aunt's farm in Widgee, Queensland when he was 6. The local school had only 80 students from grades 1 to 7, and he adapted as best as he could. At age 10, they moved again to a town called Chinchilla in south west Queensland, where his stepdad had been working on drilling rigs. Bud was bullied throughout school and found relief in working and shooting. He was always working for friends and family, competing in various shooting competitions, and winning multiple medals.

After year 10, Bud left home and hitchhiked all over Australia, working many different jobs—on fishing boats in Exmouth and cattle stations in Port Hedland and he even offered contract shooting services in multiple states for feral animals. At sixteen and a half, he started his journey by joining the Royal Australian Navy as a Marine Technician. With his shooting and bush skills, the army came knocking, and after he transferred to the army, he broke his spine at age 21 and was medically discharged. Over the years he also conducted contract security, training and teaching his skills in precision shooting. It was a blessing for him to meet his wife, Jamie, the day he was discharged while passing through Brisbane, Queensland.

It was 2007/2008, the Global Financial Crisis hit, and after having initial spinal surgeries, Bud couldn't find work anywhere. With their backs against the wall and only $38 in the bank, he and Jamie started their own business consulting mining companies on Indigenous Affairs and Veteran Employment. Within 18 months, the business had grown to consult in Mining Tenements, exploration, cultural heritage and land use agreements. Commercial negotiations were next on the cards, and soon they had 34 staff advising businesses on how to invest in real estate and manage shutdowns and mining operations.

At 29, he sold off the contracts, shut the company down, and joined the Department of Corrections to learn how people think and negotiate better when the situation turns south. After four years of managing and negotiating with prisoners, it was time to start another consultancy running mining shutdowns and helping business owners increase the performance of their struggling companies.

2019 - COVID hit and the world plunged into never-ending lockdowns and border closures, grounding Bud at home in Queensland. By this stage, his wife Jamie had been managing real estate agencies for 14 years, and in 2020, they opened Streten Global Investments, Streten Property Group and Streten Real Estate and kicked off their agency. Bud and

Jamie were fed up with how ordinary people were mistreated and taken advantage of in the real estate sector. With Jamie's real estate experience and Bud's experience in business and investing in real estate, it made perfect sense to start this business.

Bud has been helping people and businesses invest in real estate for the last 15 years and continues to speak on behalf of some of our biggest banks, financial advisors and seminars. Due to his injuries from the navy and army, he has had 11 more spinal surgeries and procedures since 2020, but he hasn't allowed these challenges to slow him down and stop him from writing this book to help people understand real estate.

Chapter 2
What is your strategy?

Strong capital gains

Capital gains are where your property's value increases over time; the higher and faster the growth, the stronger it is. As an example, if you buy your property for $450,000 and twelve months later it is worth $490,000, you have an equity growth of $40,000. Really if you think about it, you need to pay for living regardless of the home, so capital gains are a bonus!

You will naturally find more capital gains in houses over units, with some exceptions. It is common to find that rental yields are relatively small—from 4% to 6% in these properties compared to their counterparts. Each country has its own rules concerning capital gains and how they treat them. Here in Australia, how they tax your capital gains is relevant to the amount of time you have owned the property and if it was your principal place of residence. The rules are complex, but briefly, if you have owned your home for less than twelve months and it was not your principal place of residence, you will be taxed 45% of the capital gains you have made. If you are an individual (not a company) and have owned the property for more than twelve months, you qualify for a 50% discount. As I stated before, it is much more complex and intricate than this, but it gives you a basic understanding of it.

High Rental Yield

A good rental yield is between 7% and 8% return. Higher than this is excellent and is where you can start noticing the passive income that it can provide. When hunting for high rental yields, you are on the hunt for areas with easy access to services, schools, public transport and places of work. These properties are usually apartments or townhouses and have a slower capital gain but a lower initial purchase price. Be careful, though, as corporate fees can strike that excellent gross yield into a dismal net one. When in a high rental yield, you may be positively geared and need to declare that profit along with your income and be taxed on it. As mentioned in other areas of this book, having a good accountant on your team will help you understand your tax implications and what is suitable for your income.

Renovate

Forcing equity is an excellent strategy if you have managed to put the right people around you as a team. It can be very lucrative; however, you can lose it all on one project, so always ensure you have the right advice and the quickest way to force the equity is by renovating. Buying, renovating and then selling is a strategy that I use and thoroughly enjoy, even for my clients. My wife Jamie manages the design and renovations and I get to watch her create something from nothing. Once again, you need to be careful if inexperienced as the hidden costs can rapidly get out of control, and you have that capital gains tax lurking as well. Below are just two examples of the flips we have done.

Example 1. – Gold Coast, Queensland Australia (Buy and Sell)

- 2 Bed 1 Bath apartment on the seventh floor
- Purchase price: $630,000
- Settling costs: $16,300
- Renovations: $19,600 (paint, flooring, furniture and Repairs)
- Total: $665,900
- Sale price: $787,000
- Fewer sales capital gains tax: $24,220
- Profit: $96,880

Example 2 – Bellmere, Queensland Australia (Buy and hold)

- 3 bed 1 bath house on a 600m^2 block
- Purchase cost: $405,000
- Market value: $435,000 (already made gains in the buy)
- Settlement costs: $14,200

- Renovations: $45,000 (converted to a 4 bed 2 bath, new kitchen, floors, ensuite and laundry)
- New market value: $620,000
- Capital gains: $170,000

Chapter 3
Build Your Team

When you are finally ready to make your start in the real estate world it is extremely helpful to build your power team. When using professionals and receiving their advice, you're turning your zero experience into years of combined knowledge of thousands of property transactions. Let that sink in for a moment.

When assembling a power team, there are five main professionals you should include:

1. Buyer's agent.
2. Lending manager.
3. Conveyancer.
4. Accountant.
5. Building and pest inspector.

Buyer's Agent

With all the self-help websites and YouTube videos, you may be asking yourself, "are real estate agents still worth it or are they a bygone service?" By representing yourself in buying or selling, you will save yourself the commission fee, which can be a decent chunk of change. However, do you understand the work that a good agent does to earn that commission and what information they have access to and reach in local areas? If you decide to go at it yourself without help, you may end up spending or losing out on more than the agent's commission. Buying or selling a home is an emotional rollercoaster and a major financial one at that. Let's talk about why you should consider an agent.

A primary role of a real estate agent is to represent you as a client and liaise with other buyers, sellers and agents, which means that they will usually have access to a range of properties that other agents listed. While achieving your goals and strategies, a buyer's agent understands how to bring a deal together. A good buyer's agent will sit down with you and determine what you are trying to achieve by buying a property. In most cases, people do not fully understand what they want or why they are doing it, with the typical answers being "Because I want to own my own home" or "I am sick of renting." When people answer, "Because I want to use real estate to grow my wealth," they still don't understand what they said. While there are many strategies to adopt when investing in real estate, I only reference the two main strategies that most people fall into:

1. Capital Growth
2. Properties with higher capital growth are usually houses in more desirable areas and will often not have a high rental yield.

3. Yield
4. Properties with high rental yields are typically apartments or townhouses, and their capital growth is usually a lot slower.

The process of a buyer's agent covers many areas, which we will look at below.

Strategy

A buyer's agent will meet with you and have a conversation about what you are trying to achieve and look at your overall picture to help you decide which of these strategies best works for you.

Legal

The buyer's agent will discuss their fees and what level of service you need and then walk you through the contract, which in Queensland is called a Form 6. You can use a buyer's agent to provide a full search-to-settlement service or do as little as representing you by bidding at an auction. Most buyers' agents will charge a percentage of the home's purchase price as their commission, which could be 2.2%. Making up part of this overall commission will be an engagement fee which varies from $1,100.00 to $3,300.00 and is there to cover the agent's upfront costs whilst they start their service. This engagement fee will make more sense as we go through the process. Once you have agreed on the service terms and conditions, signing the contract will allow the agent to act on your behalf to find you a property.

Finance

When using the complete services of some buyer's agents, they can even accompany you to your pre-approval bank appointments so that the lender's process doesn't make you feel intimidated and you become acquainted with your lender, which comes in handy later in the process. It is a good idea for your buyer's agent to have a good relationship with your lender as it makes the process significantly smoother and less stressful when everyone is on the same page. At this stage, your buyer's agent will understand what they must work with as a budget for finding you your new property and what restrictions the lender may have. An example of this may be that the lender does not like to buy at auctions. Another critical piece of information your buyer's agent will acquire from your lender is the desired timeframe they can work with as your finance clause on the contract of sale. Most lenders require their clients to have a 14 to 21 Day finance clause on the contract of sale. I have an excellent relationship with my lending managers allowing me to undercut competitors' contracts by only having a 7-day finance clause, giving my clients the edge with the selling agent.

The Search

When searching for properties, a buyer's agent will use multiple software programs that alert them when properties that match your requirements become available. They then conduct all the background research on the properties, with many applying over 50 layers to each property to shortlist them. A few of these layers are:

- Easements.
- Bushfire threats.
- Floods.
- Nearby development applications.
- Schools.
- Public transport.
- Development potential.
- Council overlays.
- Traffic density and flow.
- Suburb growth forecasts.

Depending on your location, you can expect your buyer's agent to process around 50 properties to narrow it down to two or three to present and arrange inspections. How long would it take you to search, ring selling agents and cross-reference 50 properties with things you may not even have access to? The engagement fee we mentioned earlier starts to come into clarity as it takes a tremendous amount of person-hours and resources to even get to this point. If you decide not to buy a property, the agent hasn't wasted their time and resources.

Inspection

When the list has been narrowed down to just a few properties and presented to you, you and your agent will visit the property and determine whether it suits you and your family. For the property to get to this stage, it already suits your strategy and criteria, but you still need to feel comfortable and like it. We cover property inspections in more detail in chapter nine of this book.

Negotiations

One of the benefits of having an agent is their negotiating abilities. They negotiate many times a year compared to the average person who only buys a house twice or three times in their lifetime. Making offers and negotiating contracts can cost you immensely if you do not know what you are doing. A buyer's agent will work with your lender and conveyancer to represent you, ensuring that your best interest is in all conditions and prices.

Contract conditions

When drawing up the contract of sale with the selling agent, there will be conditions that your agent would have included. I cover the contract and conditions in another chapter; however, in this phase, your buyer's agent will ensure that everything needed to satisfy these conditions is organised and carried out.

Lending Manager

Having your lending manager as part of your power team enables you to move more efficiently when making informed decisions. You know exactly where you stand and what your borrowing capacity is. As discussed earlier, creating that rapport with your lending manager can differ between a 21-day and a 7-day finance clause and how smoothly your application will process. The length of your financial clause is a crucial point to consider when there are multiple offers on a property with the same finance conditions where the others have only access to 14 or 21-day finance. I cover mortgages, loans and pre-approvals in chapter four, finance.

Conveyancer

Conveyancing is the process of transferring ownership of a land's legal title to the new owner; this can be a person or entity.

I highly advise against attempting to do this alone as the legal work involved is complex. Diligently ensuring that nothing is left out or overlooked is crucial, and I do not envy a conveyancer's position.

There is a lot of work involved in transferring a title and ownership of a property, and it generally consists of three stages:

1. Pre-contract.
2. Pre-completion.
3. Post-completion.

A significant part of the conveyancer's role is protecting your interest in the property's contract of sale. A conveyancer also ensures that all parties know the conditions and dates required to be met or satisfied. These dates are known as the "critical dates" and a conveyancer helps you prepare for these dates. They are in regular contact with the other party's conveyancer dealing with all the issues that pop up and need addressing. If you fill the forms out yourself and make a mistake, you could lose the contract and lose your deposit. If you engage a conveyancer and then they make a mistake, at least they have professional indemnity you can claim.

What is a conveyancer?

A conveyancer is a licensed professional who provides information and advice about a property sale. Conveyancers don't have to be solicitors, although many are and undertake property law. I always strongly recommend that you engage a conveyancer when you are:

- Selling or buying a property.
- Updating a title.
- Conducting a subdivision.
- Changing, removing or registering an easement.

Financial Advisor

Financial advisors are a crucial part of your team for many reasons, both before buying a property and after.

Before buying a property, a financial advisor can help you strategise to save for your deposit and a possible comfortable loan amount. You can also use online home loan calculators to work out the maximum you could borrow, but they often do not consider your other life goals, such as planning to start a family.

After buying your property and the loan repayments commence, a financial advisor can help you develop ways to leverage or maximise your financial position. Maybe you want to go out and buy a new car, but after you run that idea past your advisor, you realise that if you wait twelve months, you will be in a far better place to ride out any hardships you may encounter, such as time off due to a global pandemic.

Bullets from Bud

- Physically meet with your lending manager to engage that connection.
- The right buyer's agent will more than pay for themselves.
- Ask around about conveyancers, especially from your agent and lending manager.
- Ensure that your financial advisor aligns with your goals.

Chapter 4
Finance

Money truly makes the world go around, and nowhere more so than in real estate. It talks about what and where you can buy, and it speaks volumes about your aspirations and motivations. In the case of first-home buyers, spending power will be the most significant single factor in determining which house to buy. Therefore, it's vital to decide on your future lifestyle by aligning your wants and needs with your budget. Even if your bank balance is less than you would hope, there is never a better time than the present to begin your home-buying journey.

Create a business plan and mission statement, declaring in writing what you want to achieve and in what timeframe, why you are chasing this goal, and how you intend to do so. Once you are happy with your mission statement, display it in a prominent position to remind you constantly about your priorities, should the motivation start to wane. If you are yet to start saving, write down a monthly budget, and stick to it. Writing your budget should incorporate all your income and expenditure. Pay particular attention to debt reduction, savings, rent, loan and credit card repayments, commitments to food, clothing, entertainment and holidays, phone and utility expenses, motor vehicle costs and any other incidentals that affect your bottom line.

As the moneysmart.gov.au and sorted.org.nz websites outline, saving can be a matter of giving up your daily coffee, making your lunch at home, cutting up your credit card, and op-shopping.

To ensure your goal remains attainable, you can download free apps, such as TrackMySpend and Booster's mybudgetpal. When the deposit is gradually taking shape, get the green light for your house hunting from lenders by gaining pre-approval.

Get a ballpark figure of borrowing capacity using an online loan calculator. Then make an appointment with a lender to learn about types of loans, fees, repayments and the First Homeowner Grant.

This amount, which usually applies for a set time, uses a limit to what you can borrow. But it also allows prospective buyers to put their plans into action. Saving requires immense discipline to reach your goal, but it is worth reminding yourself exactly of your priorities.

Besides the sale price, the not-insubstantial matters of stamp duty, settlement and mortgage costs, home insurance, removalist costs and conveyancing are also due, the sum of which can surprise first-time buyers. Factor in a contingency fund for emergencies, such as ovens, air conditioners or water heaters breaking down.

Homeownership can be extremely rewarding, but it brings with it great responsibility. If the finances have ticked the boxes, you are a winner. But if the emotions and finances do not balance out, it will pay to steer clear, at least for now. Living it up and home buying are not necessarily compatible, but it is possible to enjoy the best of both worlds if you plan well.

What is a mortgage?

A mortgage is mistakenly referred to as a loan; however, this is not the case. A mortgage is an encumbrance over a property that a lender has typically written a loan against. We will talk about the home loan, which is a loan used to buy or maintain a home, land or another real estate type. The borrower agrees to pay the lender back over time, usually in a series of regular payments divided into principal and interest. The property serves as collateral for the lender to secure the loan. A borrower must apply for a home loan through a bank or home loan broker and must meet several requirements, including minimum credit scores and deposits. Home loan applications undergo a rigorous underwriting process before they are approved for the borrower. Home loan types vary based on borrowers' needs, such as variables and fixed-rate loans.

Home loans that originated from home loan brokers reached a record high in the fourth quarter of 2020, according to Brokr Home Loans. CoreLogic examined data that the Mortgage & Finance of Australia commissioned and these data demonstrated that 18 leading aggregators settled new home loans valued at $57.47 Billion. Before choosing whom to lend from, research their repayment methods, reliability and reputation.

Bill Gates famously once said, "With great wealth comes great responsibility."

Pulling the trigger on a home loan can appear overwhelming, especially if it is your first, so understanding how one works should be at the top of your list. Friends and family can answer some questions; however, it is always a good idea to learn from a professional. Therefore, organise a time to speak with a home loan broker, bank, accountant or financial advisor. Many of these professionals will hold free "information nights" that cover a lot of information, so make sure you register for one.

Between work, family, and social media, we all live hectic lives and will not have a chance to get to the broker or bank. Many institutions - including Brokr Home loans, Commonwealth Bank and Bank of Queensland - can send a mobile lender or broker to visit you at home or work and discuss your needs.

Specialist home loan brokers, such as Brokr, RAMS and Aussie Home Loans, are gaining popularity. A bank may offer three to five home lending products; however, they may not suit your situation incurring many visits to different banks and multiple hits on your credit file. Mortgage brokers have access to many lenders; Brokr currently has access to 32 lenders and understands which one would suit your needs.

The loan that suits you best may not have the lowest

interest rate on many occasions. The features and services are much more important factors. For instance, you won't be able to make additional repayments on many of the cheaper fixed-rate loans. In addition to this, the "cut-rate" loans typically have the highest application fees.

When trying to decide which loan product is right for you, it will most likely have a particular combination of features, services and rates. Unfortunately for you, the right loan is usually never the first one you find on Google. The brokers I mentioned earlier may come into your strategy as they understand their lenders' products and your situation to marry up the right combinations for you.

Bullets from Bud

- You may need to rely on the judgement of your lender being in your best interest. Taking out a home loan is less risky than investing because the lender gives you money. Therefore, choose a lending institution with a record of ethical behaviour and you'll have peace of mind concerning your finances.
- Knowledge is key.
- Have the lender come to you.
- Consider the alternatives.
- Don't judge a loan by its interest rate.

Essential Pre-Purchasing Costs To Account For

When people think of the costs of buying a house, they typically think of a deposit, maybe conveyancer costs or removalists. Unfortunately, the list is much more extensive, and many have fallen victim to this. It is an all too familiar scene of people having to pay for many of these costs on high-interest credit cards due to not being aware of or budgeting for them.

Pre-purchase costs can quickly add up to 9% of the purchase price of an average family home. Some typically only occur once over your journey of finding a home, as they happen after you have signed a contract, such as conveyancing, stamp duty and mortgage costs. Be sure to do your homework and narrow down the properties you want to sign a contract on as costs like building and pest inspections and valuations occur with each property.

Essential fees to consider when building your budget.

- Property.
- Stamp duty — a tax on the property's value paid at the time of purchase to the state or territory government.
- Lenders Mortgage Insurance — usually paid if a mortgage exceeds 80 percent of the property value.
- Application fees — paid to the lender to meet legal, valuation and administration.
- Loan Establishment Fee.

- Inspections — including pest inspection, council building certificate, building inspection and land surveys.
- Contract examination incurs the solicitor's fees for inspecting the property contract.
- Conveyancing — The legal process of enabling the transfer of property ownership.
- Insurance — building and contents.
- Relocation — such as moving costs and utility deposits
- Repairs — the cost of essential property repairs.

The above list represents some of the essential pre-purchasing costs; however, they don't stop there. Other areas to consider may include:

Minor defects such as grout in the bathroom or leaking gutters are common, especially in buildings over ten years old. Significant flaws can be present and could even result from a smaller one like subsidence due to leaking gutters or downpipes pooling water where they shouldn't.

Pre-purchase building and pest inspections are necessary, and we will cover these a little more in-depth in chapter 13; however, sending an expert to five or six properties you have your eye on can become quite expensive. To negate this, it pays to learn the basics quickly to keep a property on or off your shortlist. A few problems to train your eager eyes to keep a lookout for are rising or falling damp, which can appear as bubbling paint, dark patches around the cornices or distinctive smells. Bouncy floors can be poor ventilation and dark patches on the ceiling can indicate plaster repairs. Building inspections can range from $200 to $600 per inspection on a typical family home.

Before a lender finalises or gives you money against the property, they will evaluate it to ensure it is worth what you have offered to pay. This can become expensive if you buy at an auction or bid on multiple properties. The costs for the evaluation can vary, so it is best to understand what that is from your lender so that you can factor it in when the time comes.

Bullets from Bud

- Budget for 10% of the purchase price; that way, you should never be surprised.
- Educate yourself first before looking at properties so you can quickly include or exclude homes on your shortlist.
- Write a spreadsheet of costs to make it quick to change on the run.
- Tap into your local real estate agents to understand property values in the area; this way, there are no surprises come evaluation day.

Lenders Mortgage Insurance (LMI)

Lender's mortgage insurance was first introduced to Australia in 1965 and created more opportunities for the average person to obtain a home loan. In addition, it encouraged lenders to lower their interest rates.

Lender's mortgage insurance is an insurance policy that

covers the **lender** against the losses they may incur if the borrower can no longer pay loan repayments; this is what they call a default. The lender's mortgage insurance should not be confused with a mortgage protection insurance product that covers you, the borrower, in the cases of death, sickness, unemployment or disability.

If a borrower defaults on their mortgage, the lender's mortgage insurance allows them to recover what is owed to them by **repossessing the property**. But if the property's value is less than the loan, the lender can suffer a loss, and it is this risk that the lender's mortgage insurance covers. With this risk passed on to the lender's mortgage insurer, lenders are more willing to approve loans at a higher **loan-to-value ratio** (LVR); this can often be up to a maximum of 95% of the property's value or sale price (whichever is lower).

Interest Rates

Unless you have cash and want to use it, you will require a loan from a lender to purchase your property. The lender will loan around 80%-90% of the value to buy your new home in most cases. When borrowing money from a lender, the amount you borrow is called the "Principal", and the interest rate is the annual cost of borrowing that amount. Your loan repayments cover two parts, the first is interest repayments, and the second is principal repayments. Other products, such as interest-only, exist, which I will cover a little further in the book. The most significant impact on your loan repayments will be the interest rate, which determines the overall amount you will pay back to the lender. For this reason, it is imperative to have at least a basic knowledge of how interest rates work and how they can affect your mortgage.

How is interest calculated on a home loan?

As said earlier, interest is charged when you take out a loan. The interest is presented in percentage terms and called the Annual Percentage Rate or APR. Your lender will take your loan amount and multiply it by your interest rate. The lender will then divide that figure by 365 days or 366 days in a leap year. Keep in mind that lenders calculate the APR per year.

As an example, you have a loan or a principal amount of $600,000, and your interest rate is at 2.5%. To calculate one day of interest, you would use this formula:

(Principal x rate) / 365 = interest

($600,000 x 0.025) / 365 = $41.09.

If you want to see your interest cost every month, you need to divide by 365 and then multiply by the number of days in a month. Using a home loan calculator can give you a better overview of your home loan and explore the repayment options. Most lenders will have a home loan calculator on their website.

What affects interest rates?

Lenders are a business, and they make their money on the interest they charge you. They borrow the money at one rate and lend it to you at a higher rate. When their borrowing conditions change, naturally, they will adjust their lending condition to suit. Other factors can alter the interest rates, such as

- **Purpose of the loan: Investment or Owner Occupy.**
  As the name suggests, an owner-occupied loan is a loan you obtain to buy a home to live in yourself. An investment property loan is to buy a property you intend to rent out. The critical difference between the two is the interest rate. Investment loans often have higher interest rates than owner-occupied loans.
- **Interest Rate Type: Variable vs Fixed.**
  Home loans come with either a fixed or variable rate. In a fixed-rate loan, your interest rate is locked in or "fixed" for an agreed length of time. Alternatively, a variable-rate loan changes its interest rate over time. You can split your home loan to include variable and fixed interest components to spread your interest rate risk.
- **Principal Amount:**
  The amount you borrow will affect your repayments significantly. The more you borrow, the more home loan interest you need to repay.
- **Loan Repayment Type: Principal and Interest vs Interest-Only.**
  By choosing a Principal & Interest loan, you will repay some principal each month and some interest. A principal and interest method is the most common option. On the other hand, your lender may be able to switch your loan to Interest-only repayments, where you only pay the interest on your loan. The interest-only method is for a set period,

and whilst doing so, you do not pay off the principal. While this option has lower repayments, your repayments will increase once the interest-only term ends, and you could end up paying more interest over the life of your loan.

How to reduce the amount of interest paid?

One way to reduce your overall cost is to contribute extra repayments toward your loan. The more often you pay your loan, the less interest you will pay over the life of the loan. Some lenders will have an offset account, which allows you to deposit your salary and other income to "offset" the interest. You can access this money like a standard account. When calculating your loan interest, the amount in the offset account reduces your home loan balance. An example of this is if you have a loan balance of $600,000, but you have $50,000 in your offset account, the lender will be calculating the interest on $550,000. Lastly, to reduce your interest paid to shop around, many brokers can help you identify better deals with lower interest rates. Ensure you understand the entire loan product as a lower interest rate doesn't automatically mean the best outcome.

Pre-Approval

Gaining a Pre-Approval is a crucial step when buying real estate; it lets you know how much you can borrow so you don't waste time looking at properties that are not in your budget. A Pre-Approval is also essential when making offers on properties as the selling agent's job is to get the most money for their client's property and reduce the risk to the seller of contracts falling over. If you and another person have an offer on a property and you don't have pre-approval, but your opposition does, you will not stand a chance as they do not pose an extra threat of being turned down by the lenders to buy the home. There are many aspects to a pre-approval, so let's cover a few here.

Pre-approval should be the first step in your home loan application process. It's preliminary approval from a lender saying they will give you a home loan of a specific amount, subject to certain conditions. A pre-approval does not mean that you are guaranteed a loan from that lender – it simply indicates that your application and situation fit the lender's criteria. It would be best if you gain pre-approval for a home loan before searching for a property and making an offer on it. It is the best indicator that the lender will accept your scenario, giving you the confidence to find a property and make an offer.

You will typically meet with a mortgage lending specialist when applying for pre-approval. You will find these people at the lender's branch or more lenders are providing mobile capabilities for their mortgage specialists to come to you. They will go through the application and enter all your credentials and finances.

The lender's credit department then conducts a full assessment, reviewing your documents and performing a credit check. This type of pre-approval can take a few days to be accepted and issued. This process may result in the lender undertaking a credit check against your name, leaving an enquiry on your file, so check and make sure of their intent. Many lenders can now provide pre-approval without touching your credit file; they will do the credit check after finding a property and applying for the full loan. Multiple inquiries on your credit file can affect your credit score negatively, and brokers are great at minimising this.

Pre-approvals expire,

Most lenders' pre-approvals are valid for between three and six months. The main reason for expiration dates is that a borrower's financial situation and the property market can change within these timeframes. Make sure you ask your lender what happens if you do not find a property before your pre-approval expires.

If the property is unacceptable, will my loan not be approved?

A pre-approval does not include assessing whether the lender accepts the property; this is because making an offer on a home is done after receiving pre-approval. Most pre-approvals will have a condition that the final loan is subject to a satisfactory property evaluation. Further to this, some lenders may not accept certain types of properties, like:

- Particular types of apartment blocks.
- Rural property over 50 hectares.
- Certain suburbs.
- A property with significant easements or high voltage lines close to it.

- A property that is in a poor state of repair.

Please make sure you chat with your lender about what types of properties they do not accept.

You may not be approved if your circumstances change.

After gaining your pre-approval, the lender will need to reassess your application if your financial situation changes or alters from your original application. It may mean that you can no longer afford the repayments on your proposed loan. Some examples of these changes could include:

- Changed jobs.
- You go part-time or become self-employed.
- You accept a new credit card or loan.
- Increase dependents such as another child.
- Spend your deposit.
- Lenders discover loans or credit cards that you did not initially disclose.

These changes don't necessarily mean the lender will reject your application. Still, you will need to talk your lender through how these changes will affect your financial situation and ability to make the repayments. Regardless of whether your situation changes after pre-approval, you will always undergo a full assessment after you've found the property you want to buy before approving your loan.

Changes to interest rates can affect your pre-approval.

Interest rate changes are always possible whilst looking for a home after gaining pre-approval finance. The interest rates can affect your final loan approval if the interest rates rise, then your repayments will also increase, and the amount you could borrow will decrease.

Pre-approval tells sellers that you're serious about buying.

As mentioned earlier, having a pre-approval demonstrates to the selling agent that you are serious and ready to go, reducing the seller's risk of a contract falling over. It lets you put in offers on properties when you see them possibly beating your competitor and moving to your final approval quicker. The selling agent may ask you to view your pre-approval letter from the lender; this is not unusual, so don't be put back if this happens.

Chapter 5
Define Your Area

Location is key to valuable real estate. Homes in cities with little room for expansion tend to be more beneficial than those with plenty of space. Consider the accessibility, appearance and amenities of a neighbourhood and development plans.

It is all too easy when searching the many real estate listing websites to wander off into multi-million-dollar homes and dreams. Rapid clicks on the back button after seeing the repayments calculator follow this browsing. We all do this at some point in life; we even do it when looking to buy a new car or item of clothing, Watch, and the list continues. It is essential to define our criteria to avoid wasting valuable time. There are many ways to determine what area suits you to buy a home, and I like to consider the following to help me find a good area:

- Budget
- Desirability
- Work
- School

- Growth

Budget

After following the earlier chapter in this book, you would now have your pre-approval finance and know how much of the bank's money you can spend. Your budget is the most significant limiting factor of where you can buy. Many sites on the internet will advise you on what suburb's median prices match your budget. Add these suburbs to your search alerts which we will cover later. Also, look around the suburbs that are a price bracket above this and keep a keen eye out for the "worst house in the best suburb" scenario. Remember with this strategy that you will need enough budget for repairs and make the property liveable, but it is a fantastic way to force equity.

Desirability

What Does Desirability Mean?

Desirability in real estate is measured as a metric and used to describe how certain areas meet the needs of their population. We use desirability to demonstrate and understand how popular a place is with the people already living there.

We can display desirability as a ratio as some suburbs have more properties than others, so using a percentage can allow the comparison of suburbs or areas of all sizes. Let us have a look at an example,

An area with a 90/100 desirability score means that only 10% of the people residing there want to sell their homes in any given year. The other 90% of the people in that area are content and do not want to sell or relocate, demonstrating a level of desirability.

The desirability ratio does not show the people's feelings but instead shows how they think about their property and area. It measures the number of properties for sale, not the number of properties sold. It is essential to remember that it is not crucial that the property was sold, as it still shows that the area has become undesirable to that person.

The ratio shows us that some areas have more listings than others. An area or suburb with high listings means that it is not meeting the people's expectations, needs or wants. Two metrics at play correlate when assessing desirability - Buyer Willingness and Absorption. When a buyer's willingness and absorption are together, they describe how buyers feel about that area.

So why does this matter?

When people have lived in the same neighbourhood for a long time, they are satisfied with their property, whether it is their primary residence or an investment. There are many reasons for someone's situation to change. If a person loses their job or has outgrown the property with additional family members, it may cause them to sell their property and seek a more desirable area that suits their requirements. The more desirable the suburb or location, the longer people will live there as they are more comfortable. Desirability affects property prices as desirable areas will always have fewer properties listed for sale, creating greater demand and forcing prices up.

The opposite is true for the less desirable areas, there will be more properties listed, and supply will be greater, forcing prices down.

Work

If you aren't working from home and you need to commute to be physically present every day, distance matters. Anyone who enters the rat race of suburban streets and freeways to commute daily understands well that time and distance are never equal. Living 30km from your work can quickly turn into an hour's commute in traffic to and from work, racking up to 10 hours per week. When looking for a home to buy, conduct test runs from that area to your work during traffic peak hours to work out your commute times. Also, think about what type of work you are in and where this may take you. Do you travel extensively for work? Are you a truck driver who must park your truck at home?

School

Schools are often a missed topic by people without children as they usually don't understand how schools can affect the value of an area. While it may initially appear that people without children shouldn't be concerned, the quality of the schools and school catchment area can affect the property values directly. If you fall into the family with children category and intend to use the local schools, here are a few tips you can do to investigate the area further.

- Talk to neighbours in the area who also have

children.
- Go to the local playground and ask other parents.
- Ask the school for a tour.
- Talk to the P&C (PTA) or attend a meeting. At the time of writing, I am currently the president of our daughters' School P&C (PTA) and receive calls from new parents, which is good.

I live in Brisbane, Australia, and we have catchment areas for public schools, meaning if you live outside the school "Catchment Area", your child cannot attend there. Suburbs and locations within the prestige school catchment areas can skyrocket in value, with some properties worth $200,000 more than the exact property across the street due to it falling in these areas.

Growth

When a suburb turns into a hotspot, the property values can grow strongly within short periods; if you learn how to find them, you can give your portfolio's equity a substantial head start. Historically speaking, hotspot suburbs usually associate themselves with vital industry areas such as mining, which go up and down to extremes. Avoiding these areas is a good idea if you are not a seasoned investor.

Genuine hotspot suburbs that retain their value, or close to it, when they rise are the areas that you should learn to identify. You may get frustrated if you try to do this yourself. You will usually hear about these areas after they have already boomed and would be buying at the peak; we suggest building your power team to help you in these efforts. Let us look at how to identify signs of a suburb experiencing genuine growth.

Supply and demand:

The supply and demand ratio of properties in a suburb or area is one of the strongest drivers of price growth. The fewer properties on the market, the more people are willing to pay well above the asking price to secure a home in that area. When demand outweighs supply, it is called a seller's market. Low-interest rates create more buyers, lack of developments in a suburb, or a general change in a population's situation can be just a few factors in causing a seller's market. We saw this in the COVID-19 global pandemic, which created an environment where people worked from home and job uncertainty, making people hold onto their homes.

- Look for areas where rental yield increases; this indicates a location desirable to renters. When renters buy a home, they usually buy within the area they already live.
- A rising population is also a good indicator. Property prices will increase when the increasing population combines with rising income and low supply.
- Look at the demographics of the people moving into an area. The statement relates to the average and not the few, but suburbs with a median age of 35 tend to gentrify quicker. They tend to have more income, increasing affordability when buying or

renting properties.

Gentrification:

I am sure we have all seen suburbs that once were areas where we locked the doors driving through them but now seem to be surging ahead in property prices. When a suburb experiences a change in demographics and landscape, it usually changes the perception of that suburb. The suburbs' desirability goes up and this increases housing prices.

- Identify affordable suburbs and areas that interest you.
- Research the property prices for the last two to three years.
- If a slow price increase is noted, look at the demographic of the area. Noticing an expansion of a younger population with good incomes demonstrates signs that the suburb is about to be gentrified.
- Keep an eye out for increased renovating or building of properties.
- Are there new shops and cafes opening? If so, these business owners have most likely spent a significant amount of time and money researching the area before they decided to open up there.

The ripple effect:

Not everybody can afford to buy in the booming hotspot suburbs, or you may have missed out, and it is at its peak. If this is you, then studying the ripple effect will help dramatically. Riding the ripple effect is where using the local agents' knowledge comes in, as it requires timing. The timing refers to the property cycle of the area to maximise your chances of getting in before you miss out.

- Research the surrounding suburbs of a hotspot and measure property values by comparing median prices.
- If the variation is more significant than 5%, this suburb is likely playing catch up with the hotspot.
- Research median price trends closely every quarter, and once you are sure the property cycle has kicked off, start looking for properties within the budget as close to the growth as possible.
- If the budget allows, buy within the twelve-kilometre CBD range as growth is guaranteed to ripple this far.

Large infrastructure projects:

When large-scaled infrastructure projects get underway, it is a good sign that the area will experience a sharp rise in property prices. People come in droves for jobs, and the housing demand increases. The preference when looking for projects is those that have already started, as we all know the funding is dependent on politicians' election promises.

Chapter 6
Define Your Property

You won't find any argument against the statement that Australia has one of the most expensive housing markets globally, even when you measure it against our relative income. These prices are especially true in our capital cities, and at the time of writing, the average price per square metre of housing is:

- Australia: AUD 8470.00
- The United States of America: AUD 2541.00
- The United Kingdom: AUD 3060.05

Naturally, there are many categories to choose from when looking to buy, depending on budget, lifestyle, situation and location. Here in Australia, we usually define properties by six categories, they may call them different words around the world, but they are all similar. In Australia, we would call it an apartment, and in the United States, we would call it a condominium. The six categories are.

- House
- Terrace House
- Semi-detached House
- Duplex
- Townhouse
- Apartments and units

This chapter will explain each category in-depth and what makes them unique to understand better when choosing which is suitable for you. Importantly, it is wise to realise that definitions of categories written here are what the public understands and recognises; however, their descriptions may change from state to state and within individual councils.

House:

Also called a stand-alone house, it is a freestanding house in which the buyers usually own the land and any other dwellings, such as sheds, within its boundaries. Depending on planning codes, there may be other liveable dwellings on the same property title, such as a granny flat. The size of the block of land or "Lots" that the house sits on can vary broadly, and typically the further out from a CBD you get, the larger the standard suburban block is. The larger lot sizes aren't to be taken for a given in the outer suburbs as many still have tiny lot sizes available.

Often considered the most flexible property type, you can renovate, extend or knockdown for further development depending on the local council planning codes and regulations. The stand-alone house with a yard, gardens to play in, and maybe even an outdoor entertaining area may suit bigger families with younger children. They are also usually more expensive to maintain and operate, with electricity bills, insurance and council rates typically more significant than the other property types.

A stand-alone house also, on average, appreciates faster in capital gains than medium and high-density properties.

Terraces:

Typically found in the inner city, terraces increased in the late 1800s and early 1900s before falling out of favour in the mid-1900s. Back in fashion today, both for their relative affordability and their promise of low-maintenance living close to amenities, older terraces are being renovated, and new-style terraces are increasingly making their way into master-planned communities.

Ranging from a single storey to four storeys in height, often with two to four bedrooms, front and back gardens or courtyards, terraces are rarely freestanding but share party walls more often.

Older terrace stock tends to come with a Freehold Title, which means you own the property's land. At the same time, newer developments may be strata-titled, especially if they have access to communal facilities.

Semi-Detached House:

Typically, a semi-detached house shares one common wall with the neighbouring house and was once used as an affordable alternative to the stand-alone house. Commonly built around the 1900 mark, many semi-detached houses are old and have been renovated or extended, keeping the period features and facade. Even today, they can be more affordable with a minimal footprint and typically use their backyard as off-street parking. Erected in 1988, you can find a fine example of how these beautiful homes made a comeback along Gregory Terrace in Spring Hill, Brisbane.

Duplex:

A duplex is a dwelling containing two homes sharing a common central wall and will exist as either one or two separate titles. The two houses are independent in a duplex with their entries and amenities. If they are on one title, they must both be sold together instead of having them on two titles, which allows them to be bought and sold separately. Although a body corporate is not used in these situations, the owners must agree on certain items such as building insurance policies that cover both halves of the dwelling.

There are many benefits for both owner-occupiers and investors when buying a duplex. If you're an owner-occupier, a massive attraction to a duplex usually is its price which can often be as little as half of what you would pay for a similar stand-alone house. This means that those first home buyers and anyone on a tight budget can afford a property in the more desirable areas without sacrificing a lifestyle. I have often sold people's homes when they are getting older and want to downsize, and often, I have helped them find a duplex to buy.

When building a duplex, an investor will achieve nearly

the exact rental yield compared to subdividing the land and building two houses but without the extra costs involved. It also means that the investor will have two rental incomes from one asset and title. When assessing suburbs and locations with an older or ageing population, I usually hunt around for suitable blocks for developing and building duplexes. I know they will cost less to produce and sell quickly.

A duplex means that you can get into better locations a lot cheaper than buying a house out of budget. It is also cheaper to live in and needs less maintenance. The payoff is losing a little privacy with the shared common wall. However, remember that these common walls are usually thicker and more insulated to help with this issue.

Townhouse:

You can find townhouses as multistorey, either attached or freestanding and usually within a complex of three or more others. A townhouse is self-contained, and the owners typically own the dwelling but share the ownership of the land they sit on and any other communal property with the other owners within the complex. Townhouses will often have a shared courtyard, outdoor dining area, and maybe a pool and garages or carports for parking. Since most townhouses are strata-titled, there is usually a body corporate in operation, which means that owners pay an annual fee for the maintenance and repairs of the premise and structures.

The body corporate charges and what they are responsible for covering varies between sites. You can request a body corporate disclosure statement that outlines what money they have for repairs, the annual fees, and what they cover for repairs and maintenance. Freehold townhouses exist and have become more popular, but strata-titled townhouses are still the majority. When I first met my wife, we moved into a three-storey townhouse in Ascot, Brisbane. At this time, I had a culture shock since I was used to wide-open acres of land. I love buying and selling townhouses as the people who want them are usually young professionals full of energy or young couples starting with what they can afford.

Apartments:

Apartments, also called units, are usually found in the form of a building with multiple dwellings and fall in the medium to high-density zones. An apartment building is similar to a townhouse where there is typically a body corporate that manages the day-to-day operations of the building; this includes any maintenance and repairs to common areas. Body corporate fees vary greatly depending on location and facilities. Some apartment buildings are only single- or two-story walk-ups and can have over 60-storey buildings in our cities.

Apartments offer great living for those who lead busy lives, be they a student or career-driven people. They are low maintenance, and usually close to most public transport and amenities. Apartments have a much slower capital growth rate than a house or duplex but, as a trade-off, have higher rental yields if you are an investor. What you lose in having to contribute to an annual body corporate fee, you can gain in fewer commute times, fewer maintenance costs, and less stress.

Chapter 7
Starting Your Search

Parameters:

Many people know what they want to buy for their first or next property. To start your property search, you need to decide about location and property type, the number of bedrooms, bathrooms and maybe even a minimum yard size. These may change a little as you make compromises here and there, but it serves as the basis so you can narrow it down as quickly as possible when you search online.

Everyone and every home are different, so ensuring that you have a solid idea of what you are after is crucial. So many people have said that the struggle is to find what they are after; if it is a seller's market, they miss out, and if it is a buyer's market, they are overwhelmed. Tailoring your property search is necessary and can save you months of misery, disappointment and wasted weekends spent at open homes.

It is now time to focus on the search and where things get interesting. This stage is where, if you are a couple or partners, two human beings must agree on what they both want. Things can get a little frustrating and heated as neither side wants to compromise on their wants or perceived needs. One partner may wish to have an open-plan kitchen, and the other may like the island bench idea. This indifference is an unequivocal statement, but you will be surprised by how little something must be to cause a quarrel.

The "Must-haves" and the "Nice-to-have" are essential and writing them down in a list form to take you to inspections always helps you from becoming caught up in the moment of the property. It happens to the best of us so ask yourself, have you ever noticed when looking at a property or car that you question your memory of the item and things you were supposed to look at when you leave?

When searching for my next properties, I break down my search into groups; some groups are not relevant to all searches depending on your purpose; i.e., occupier, investor or developer. These groups are what you will enter as your parameters on the search engines online.

- Dwelling type, size and specifications.
- Location.
- Lot size.
- Development potential.
- Price and budget range.

You may change what you find essential when looking for a property if you understand why you are making that decision and its impact on the overall position you are aiming for. Remember that the longer your search goes on, the more disheartened you will feel, and you will lose sight of the must-haves. When people get desperate and buy a property that is outside their requirements most of the time, they end up selling the property prematurely and getting into a worse situation than when they initially bought it.

Alerts:

Alerts are critical in a seller's market due to how quickly properties are selling on the market. Jumping on your local real estate websites once a week is not enough, and you will miss out repeatedly. By setting up alerts on these websites, you will receive notifications as soon as a property that meets your criteria is listed, saving you a lot of time. Most websites are free and require you to sign up for an account; spending five minutes setting up will save you time in the long run. Some websites, such as www.domain.com.au here in Australia, allow agents to give early access to their properties so that people who have signed up for alerts see properties before they are listed publicly. The key here is that the fewer eyeballs that have seen the property, the better chance you will be successfully moving in.

Keeping track:

This can be tricky and can quickly become a confusing cluster of information overload, slowing you down as you try to decipher your poorly written notes. Developing

Once you start attending open homes and inspections, the features of each property will begin to blur together. Taking a camera with you and developing a good spreadsheet on a program such as Microsoft Excel can be a real advantage and ensures accuracy. Please take a photo outside the property and assign it to the register for quick reference; make notes on an inspection sheet as you walk through it. The inspection sheet helps you remember what features were there and what you felt while touring the home and can be married against the "Keeping Track" register.

If you want to use my templates, you can find them at www.stretenpropertygroup.com.au/templates. Find the Keeping Track and Listing sheet file and download it.

Chapter 8
Shortlisting Your Search

On average, when I hunt for my next property, I will look at and evaluate well over fifty properties. It would be impossible to attend fifty open homes and inspections, so how do I shortlist the properties? The answer to this question is to "Strikeout, not count in." The previous chapter covered the initial property search and criteria. That is where you count properties not here. Below is how I shortlist my potential properties.

Most properties will have something about them that fails the shortlist test; this may be as simple as the property being under contract and the agent hasn't updated the listing. Make sure you group the properties by the agent, as you can look silly repeatedly calling the same agent six times in two hours. Go through and phone every agent on every property; if they don't answer, always leave a voicemail with what property you are interested in, your contract conditions, and the best way to contact me. Ensure you follow the voice message or answer phone calls with an email mentioning the property and contract conditions. You will strike out half of your list by conducting the above. Many properties have already gone under contract or sold. In other cases, the seller's ideal contract conditions aren't suitable, or other offers have already gone above your budget.

Once you have your revised list of around twenty to twenty-five remaining properties, quickly revisit the listings to refresh your memory on each property. Phone back the selling agent of each property and put an offer in; yes, that is correct, site unseen. You can revise your offer or pull it completely once you have inspected the property. Make sure you follow up your calls with an email outlining your conversation with the selling agent. The idea here is to be at the forefront of the listing and demonstrate that you are a lower risk to the seller. When I conduct open homes and when buyers call me, discuss their potential contract conditions and place an offer on a property, I tend to remember who they are. Depending on their attitude, if their offer and contract conditions are the same as another buyer and both cannot go any higher, I will lean toward the person I remember and have started a rapport with. Research the address against overlays such as flood, fire, traffic maps and any other data you can get your hands on, and again, another ten or so properties will strike off the list.

With the ten properties you have left, it is time to arrange private inspections and attend open homes. Ten properties are my limit for inspecting any more than this, and you will not be able to cover or be present at all the showings. Once you have walked through the properties, ensuring you fill in your trusty listings sheet, you will realise that you will only have about three properties left on your keeping track register. So why do the last seven or so properties get struck out? Because there are factors that internet and window listings cannot describe accurately, such as people using the street as a suburb shortcut, noise or nasty sun glare.

- Wow! you quickly went from fifty properties to just three; now that is shortlisting. With your remaining three properties, this is what you are going to do.
- Email the agent with the revised offer and contract conditions. When sending this email, copy your team into this and make sure that it is CC, not BCC, as you want the selling agent to see that you are highly organised, have all your team in place and represent a lower risk than any other buyer with whom they are talking. Why is being a lower risk to the seller a good thing? Because if you fall over on your contract, you will create long delays, and the selling agent must renegotiate the sale with another buyer.
- Phone the selling agents to confirm they have received your email. You would be surprised at how many potential buyers' emails end up in my junk file, and I never see them.

Always ask the selling agent for their timeline and expectations. Their answer will tell you when to follow up again and could look like this.

"I will be taking all offers to the sellers on close of business Wednesday, and I will be advising buyers on Thursday with the outcome." I will cover offers and contracts in further detail in another chapter.

Chapter 9
Inspecting the Property

Conducting adequate inspections is a vital part of the journey to buying a home. You want to find a home that's a wonderful place to live and a good investment, and a thorough inspection helps gather the information you need to make the best decision. This quick guide will equip you with the fundamentals you need to get this right to narrow down the search list. Remember your listing sheet that we covered in previous chapters.

Take in the home as a whole

Walk through the whole property and think about how it feels to be there. Ask if it meets your needs and if you can see yourself living there. Use all your senses for this, not just your sight. For example, listening to the sounds of the area will give you an idea about traffic noise and neighbours.

Don't be shy – check all the nooks and crannies.

Turn on the taps to check the water pressure and any issues with leaks. Look in all the cupboards for any signs of damage or mould. Try the light switches, windows, and doors to see that everything's working as it should and look under rugs where possible to check the floors.

Don't forget to use your nose – smells give significant clues about mould and water damage issues.

Remember the things you can't see

No matter how thorough your inspection, there are things you need to be aware of before buying a home that only trained professionals can uncover. Problems such as termite infestations or issues with structural integrity can be invisible to the untrained eye.

Because of this, it's essential to organise a range of checks. These include a building inspection to evaluate the structural soundness of the property and any other features such as swimming pools, a pest inspection and a surveyor's report. These inspections come at a cost, but they are worth it to avoid far more expensive outlays down the track.

On top of seeking professional advice, you should also research the home you are interested in yourself. Look for environmental hazards that could place the property at risk and drive-up insurance costs, such as bushfires and flood zones. Check with the local council and government for zoning regulations and proposed developments that could affect your property. If the home is part of a complex, obtain a strata report and read the by-laws that apply to see that the complex is a good fit for you. Visit the neighbourhood at different times to see how traffic, noise and activity change over time.

Being thorough in your inspection will help you make the right decision when choosing the best home for you.

Chapter 10
Making an Offer

At this stage of your journey, you will have had enough of looking at houses; you would love nothing more than for your offer to be accepted and go under contract. It is a gut-wrenching feeling while waiting to hear back from the selling agent, especially when there are multiple offers on the property you have set your sights on.

Adding to the stresses and emotions of trying to buy your next home, it is devastating when your offer is not accepted and you realise that you are back on the hunt. Thankfully, there are a few things that you can learn to boost your chance of the seller accepting your offer when you are competing with others. When buying property, I use these techniques and have had great success, but remember, you still need to have all your team in place and ready.

1. **Know your limit and what the market is doing** – I'll present you with a scenario to explain this. I bought a three-bed and one-bath home in Brisbane. The asking price was $400,000 and the home

required a little work, namely painting, putting in a new carpet and fixing the kitchen. There were multiple offers around the $375,000, and I knew the house was coming in at $395,000 - $400,000 in the evaluations. I put an offer in well above asking at $405,000, crazy, right? Well, here is why I did that. It was a hot seller's market, and if I had offered $380,000, the other buyers would have been comfortable putting in counteroffers, and after going back and forth, we would have gone to $410,000 - $415,000. The reason people do this is they get to the point where they think that they are already over and start fighting for the property emotionally, leaving you well above where you want to be and out of the running. After placing a significantly higher offer of $405,000 on the property, I knew the other buyers would be too scared to go any higher as the "market value" was only $400,000. I also knew that two similar properties in the neighbourhood had just sold for $430,000, but the evaluations hadn't caught up yet. The market was also set to increase by 15% in the following 12 months, so even if I had overpaid by $5,000, the market would have caught it by the next six months. Like the point title says, know your limit and your market.

2. **Take a builder to the open home or inspection** - Find a builder that you can take with you when you inspect the property. Naturally, you will have to pay them a fee if they aren't on your team or know

them personally, but it is well worth it. Bringing the builder allows them to conduct a brief property inspection and advise you of what maintenance, repairs or renovations would most likely be up for with that property. Why not wait for the building and pest inspection? This gives you a considerable advantage over the other buyers; even though it is not a complete building and pest, the builder may give you enough information and advice to waive your contract's building and pest condition. When selling a property, the selling agent has two main jobs, which are to get the highest price possible and to reduce the exposure of the seller to risk. Not having a building and pest clause minimises the risk of the contract falling over on the seller, so it is favourable to the seller. If you decide to follow this step, make sure you have a builder with an excellent reputation in the area you want to buy the property and that they have pest experience.

3. **7-Day finance-** We mentioned above about the selling agent reducing the risk exposure to their client, the seller. The most significant risk of the contract falling over is the buyer's finance, and in a hot seller's market, cash is the least risk. However, not everyone has cash and needs to finance the property. When writing this book, the banks are asking their clients to put a 21-day finance clause on their contracts in the current market. This clause means that the buyer has 21 days from the contract date to have the finance to buy the property. The

banks must research the property within this time by conducting evaluations and processing your application, even if you are pre-approved. When you have a good relationship with your lending manager, you will be surprised at what they can do for you to speed this process up. As soon as you know you are going to put an offer in on a property, call your lending manager and give them the address so they can run a desktop evaluation to see if the figures match up. If the figures match up, they will usually let you put a 7-day finance clause instead of a 21-day, giving you an enormous advantage over the other buyers. If a contract falls over on finance, the selling agent must return to the other buyers and get them into a contract. If it has been 21-days, then the other buyers have probably already bought elsewhere and this is why seven-day finance is an advantage.

4. **Look organised and present as little risk as possible**

   The selling agent is always looking for the least resistance possible and the smoothest transaction for their client. Dress professionally at the open home and know your figures and stats when talking with the agent. When emailing your offer or communicating with the selling agent, always visibly CC your solicitor or conveyancer, lending manager, buyer's agent, builder, and whoever is on your team. Including your team in the correspondence demonstrates to the selling agent that you are organised and should have fewer setbacks than other buyers.

5. **Show your confidence at open homes and inspections**

    This step is for putting off your competition. Remember that the other buyers are in the same situation as you and have probably not received offers accepted on other homes. If you turn up well dressed with a clipboard under your arm, show confidence and converse with the showing and selling agent using their name, you will drive doubt into the other buyers with "Why do I bother when the agent knows that buyer?" Remember to be polite while doing this, as there is a fine line separating being confident and cocky.

Just because you follow, learn and deploy these techniques does not guarantee that the seller will accept your offer; however, it will put you in the front seat of the race and not in the rear.

How to Buy 1000 Bricks

Chapter 11
Contract of Sale

I am not a solicitor or conveyancer and you should seek legal advice before agreeing to a contract of sale.

Regardless of whether you are a seasoned investor or a first home buyer, you must understand the contract of sale and what it contains. I am not going into the rabbit hole in this book over contracts as they vary worldwide; instead, I am just touching the surface to make you aware of them.

A contract of sale in real estate is an official agreement between parties for the sale, purchase, and exchange of real estate. Using a bilateral contract is most common, meaning the deal is between two parties and capturing the agreement in writing. Once again, it varies on your location, but the real estate agent or conveyancers usually "draft" the contract of sale before the buyer signs it. The contract of sale is not complete until the seller has accepted and signed the contract making all parties agreeable.

If the seller does not agree to the terms in the agreement, it is not complete or binding; for example, the seller replies to your contract offer with "I will accept your offer if you change the settlement terms to 30 days." The seller would not sign the contract until it has been amended to the agreeable terms and is called a counteroffer.

The buyer and seller's conveyancer or solicitor will manage the contract of sale, keep all parties informed with details such as actual dates and ensure that all conditions and correspondence are being conducted correctly, protecting their client.

There are basic requirements that must be present to make a contract of sale valid and below are a few:

1. Must be in writing and contain all correct details.
2. A mutual agreement must be present.
3. The contract must identify the parties.
4. Agreed purchase price.
5. The property description includes, where possible, street address and title numbers.
6. Legal considerations.
7. Signatures of all parties.

This overview is a quick brief look at a contract of sale. As mentioned at the beginning of this chapter, I am not a solicitor or conveyancer, and independent legal advice is recommended.

Chapter 12
Finance Conditions

What is a finance clause in a contract of sale?

One of the most common clauses a buyer should put as a condition in the contract of sale is the finance clause. The financial clause allows the buyer time to talk with their financial institution and have their finance approved for that property. The finance clause protects the buyer from committing to buying the property if they cannot obtain the finance to buy it.

How does a finance clause work?

When submitting their offer, a buyer will nominate a timeframe they have to complete seeking their finance approval. Commonly this will usually be seven, fourteen or twenty-one days from the contract date. When making an offer, it would look like this: "Subject to xx days finance." If the buyer's finance is approved and accepts it, the buyer's conveyancer notifies the other parties that the finance clause has been satisfied.

If the buyer has not received the approval in writing within the timeframe allocated to that clause, they must seek an extension to the clause from the seller. This extension request must be made before the date stipulated in the contract of sale and is typically made through the buyer's conveyancer. If the buyer does not request an extension or the seller does not approve an extension, the buyer will breach the contract and the seller will terminate the contract. A deposit refund will vary between countries and states; however, the buyer will have their deposit returned here in Queensland, Australia. Once terminating the contract, the seller can return the property to the market to find a new buyer or reach out to other buyers who made offers.

So, what happens if the buyer does not put a finance clause in the contract of sale? Things can get very complicated and expensive if the buyer does not gain the finance to purchase the property and needs to withdraw from the contract of sale. At the very least, the buyer will lose their deposit and possibly have legal action against them. Most contracts of sale should and do have the consequences outlined in their terms and conditions. A seller may try to recover any losses due to the buyer's actions, such as fees, penalties and costs.

Requesting an extension.

I recommend that clients regularly communicate with the selling agent and allow two business days to request an extension of their finance clause due to the multiple parties involved in the transaction. The legal side of the finance clause extension can take a little time due to the two conveyancers needing to talk to each other in writing. Communicating your intentions to the selling agent allows them to prepare their client (the seller) for what they will receive from their conveyancer. This communication with the selling agent could determine if the seller accepts the finance clause extension or terminates the contract of sale.

A buyer will talk with their conveyancer to request a finance clause extension, and then the buyer's conveyancer will communicate with the seller's conveyancer. The seller's conveyancer will seek instructions from the seller and return the decision to your conveyancer, who will tell you the outcome. You can now see why it is good to allow two business days for this process.

It is common to see finance clause extension requests in a seller's market or a property boom due to the banks being well behind on their processing times. You should seek advice from your finance provider and your conveyancer about what your finance clause should state. This advice could be the difference between buying your next property or missing out.

Involve the bank.

If you are the buyer, ensure that you send the fully signed contract of sale to your finance provider as soon as possible, they can't start the process without it, and it is an easy step to forget. Remember that you will need not just your pre-approval but also a fully unconditional finance approval before advising your conveyancer that the finance clause has been satisfied. Often, your finance provider will want to send out a licensed evaluator to advise them on the value of the property they are financing you to purchase. Once again, this process takes time, so the more time you can give your lender, the better.

Reviewing your finance offer.

Once you have received your final approval for finance from the lender, go through the offer very carefully. Ensure you ask yourself these questions.

1. Does the loan term match what you originally agreed to?
2. Does the loan interest match the pre-approval interest, or is it acceptable?
3. Will the amount you borrow be enough to cover other fees such as stamp duty, legal and additional purchasing costs?

Advise your conveyancer.

What happens next once I am satisfied with the loan offer from my lender? You advise your conveyancer that you accept your loan offer and provide them with a copy of the loan offer approval from your lender. Once your conveyancer has those two things from you in writing, they will advise the seller's conveyancer that the finance clause in the contract of sale has been met and satisfied. If no other conditions remain on the sale contract, it will go unconditional.

Signing and returning the loan documents.

You probably realise that everything in a real estate transaction takes time and a lot of it. Once you have been provided with the loan documents from your lender, sign them as soon as you are satisfied and comfortable in doing so and then return them. If you leave this until the last few days before your settlement, you will not be settling as the seller will not get paid. Often, banks need up to two weeks to review your signed documents and allocate a mortgage to the property ready for settlement.

Chapter 13
Building and Pest Conditions

Building and pest inspections are an integral part of buying a home, and I recommend conducting them on your purchase. You may hear them being called a B&P for short is usually one of the two main conditions, the other being finance, you will place on your new contract of sale unless it is an auction, which means you will need to arrange for one before the auction date. If it is a standard sale and you have nominated to have a building and pest as a condition, you will need to give a period that you agree to meet and satisfy that condition. For example, your offer for the property may sound like this.

    Purchase Price: $450,000

    Deposit: $5,000

Conditions, from the date of the contract:

    Building and Pest: 14 Days

    Finance: 14 Days

Settlement: 30 Days

The above means that you will plan to have a building and pest inspection conducted and that you will notify your conveyancer if you are satisfied or not satisfied with the report within 14 days of the contract date. Remember, a building and pest inspection is not a "Pass or Fail"; instead, it is a report outlining the shape of the building and any pests such as termites. It is up to you, the buyer, to be happy with the feedback in the report. If you are comfortable and accept the condition of the property, and you notify your conveyancer about your decision, they will instruct the seller's conveyancer that this condition on the contract is now satisfied. If for whatever reason, you are not happy with the inspection report, then you can back out of the contract and your conveyancer will handle it with the seller's conveyancer.

What happens on the day of the Building and Pest Inspection?

Once you have obtained the services of a building and pest company, they will contact the selling agent to arrange a time to visit the property. There are usually two inspectors present, one for building and one for pest, and sometimes, however, one person may cover both. I highly recommend you arrange to attend the property whilst they conduct the inspections on the day. Being present allows the inspectors to explain what they see to you in simple terms, as their reports can be intimidating. We bought a property for a client in December 2021 in Bellmere, Queensland, Australia, for $30,000 less than market value due to the building and pest report sounding scary enough to warn away most! We then renovated and converted the property for them. In the end, the termite damage set our timeline back two days and our budget about $2,400, so it was well worth investigating.

Many lenders will require council building certifications as evidence of modifications or works conducted on a property. Many DIY changes can cause real problems and safety concerns with properties and can alter their value significantly. You could maybe guess where most of these issues can arise from, right? If you said kitchen, bathroom or toilet, you would be correct. Tell-tale signs are a toilet installed too close to the kitchen and DIY plumbing. Being familiar with basic planning codes will make spotting these dodgy additions straightforward. A council building inspection and land survey will set you back about $600 per property, but I see it as an insurance policy.

The pest inspector will usually carry a stick with a bit of ball on the end that they tap on the skirting, eaves, jams and walls to detect any wood rot and termite damage. Some pest inspectors will have a thermal imaging camera in their arsenal so that they can see through the walls when looking for termites. If there are any issues, they will tell you what to do.

A brick veneer home can come under attack from termites the same way an old Queenslander would, along with their other indiscriminate partners' cockroaches. Both can cause running into the thousands. However, doing a little homework and looking in the right areas will go a long way to shortlisting or dropping a property. Check roof cavities and other dark, damp places for termites and under furniture and cupboards for cockroaches. If you want to continue putting a contract on the property, organise a pest inspection for around $250 per inspection.

Chapter 14
Other Conditions

Many clauses can be found in a contract for buyers and sellers alike. The two most common ones you will see here in Australia are the subject-to-finance clause and the subject-to-building and pest inspection clause. Many situations call for additional clauses, so let us look at just a few.

- **Subject to settlement of property.**
  This clause is where the buyer has a contract on their current property and is awaiting settlement and payment.
- **Subject to foreign investment review board approval**.
  Most countries will have a similar process when a buyer or buyers are international and are not Australian citizens. In some cases, they must apply to the Foreign Investment Review Board to gain approval to buy that property. The advice is to allow forty days for this process usually.

- **Subject to termination of the prior contract.**
  You will most likely see this clause if the selling agent is prepping you as a backup buyer where the seller feels that they will be terminating the current buyer's contract.
- **Sunset clause.**
  A sunset clause specifies a date on which the seller can terminate the contract if the buyer does not meet a specific objective. An example of where you would see a sunset clause is if the contract of sale is subject to the buyer selling their current property to finance this one.
- **Due diligence.**
  This clause is used if the buyer requires further investigations on the subject property, such as town planning for development purposes. What needs investigating should set the time frame for a due diligence clause.

You can add extra clauses to an Offer as special conditions on a contract of sale. Wording these conditions is crucial to avoid disputes later in the process, so having the right advice is necessary. Both parties must accept and sign the conditions.

Chapter 15
Unconditional Contract

What is an unconditional contract

There are generally two ways you will be involved in an unconditional contract of sale. The first and most common way is when you have satisfied the conditions on your contract of sale when buying a house and your contract deems the sale "unconditional." The second way is if you enter a contract of sale as an unconditional contract from the beginning. We have covered in earlier chapters what conditions are on a contract of sale and how to satisfy them; now, let's look at when someone would enter an unconditional contract from the beginning and the risks involved.

As markets transition from a buyer's market to a seller's market, buying a property becomes increasingly complex and competitive, and people tend to miss multiple properties. When the market is in high demand for properties and stocks are low, buyers can become more willing to compromise on contract conditions giving them more bargaining power over the other buyers. Having fewer conditions on a contract can be beneficial and attractive to a seller as a buyer has less ability to get out of a contract.

Buyers still have rights under the applicable legislation; however, as the name implies, there are no conditions. An unconditional contract means that the buyer is liable to settle the property, regardless of their status on finance or if the property is physically acceptable. On the other side, an unconditional contract binds the seller to sell on the offer they accepted in the contract. Terminating the contract halfway through cannot be done easily without exceptional circumstances. Buyers will also see these contracts at auctions where the sale is final, and no conditions are on the contract.

The risks are high when entering an unconditional contract of sale. You need to understand the depth and gravity of your situation and have a particularly good conveyancer to help identify any issues. A few of the apparent risks include:

Property condition:

Real estates use professional photographers. Even though they cannot portray the property as something it is not, photos can still be deceiving. It may have underlying issues such as wood rot, termites, pests and structural problems that would otherwise be noticed in a building and pest inspection. I always recommend having the property inspected before entering an unconditional contract.

Finance

This is an obvious one; if you require borrowing money from a financial institution and have no finance clause on the contract, you are still liable to settle the property regardless of whether you don't gain finance.

Evaluation

Emotions are a funny thing, and if you allow them to rule your mind in real estate, you will find yourself justifying the "extra" money you are paying for a property. The other side of the coin is that you may be underselling your property if you are the seller, especially in a fast-paced market.

What now that your contract is unconditional?

Congratulations! You are now well on your way to settling the property into your name and beginning your next journey. It is time to finish organising your life and locking in ready to move.

Organising utilities

This is an area that many people have fallen victim to not having organised in time and are caught out with no internet. Making phone calls about your internet, power and gas seems endless, but it is essential to get this done as many of these providers can take weeks to make the transition happen. There is nothing worse than moving into your new home and having a cold shower for the first five nights while you wait for the gas to be connected; trust me, we know. I had miserable daughters and a miserable wife when I experienced this problem. Some companies provide a fee-for-service to organise all your utilities for the move.

Packing can be one of the most stressful parts of moving and can cause many arguments between family members. If you break this down into a week-by-week strategy, it can prove quite handy and accurate and even begin before buying a property. Let us break it down.

Six weeks out - Decide what you want to take with you and clean

- **Conduct a quick clean –**
  Conducting a quick clean of your home will make it easier to decide what you are taking with you to your new home.
- **Room by Room –**
  Go through each room and decide which items you will discard. Remember, the fewer items you have to move, the easier and cheaper it will be to move. Choosing items to move will also help you stay organised.
- **Gather the item you don't want to keep together**
  If it is not possible to discard your unwanted items all at once or straight away, gather them and put them out of the way to understand what you still have to move. You will be amazed at how much you won't be taking with you.

Five weeks out - Sell or discard your unwanted items

Selling your unwanted items can be a great way to help put some dollars back into the moving costs, and there are plenty of free online marketplaces that you can use in your area. People cannot resist a bargain, even if they don't need it. My wife amazes me when our girls have finished playing with a toy or have outgrown it, and she advertises it online. I look at it and ask her, "Who will buy that?" Well, she has proven me wrong every time. If you cannot sell the item, then donate it! Donating is especially helpful with furniture, and many charities will send their truck to pick it up from you and put it to effective use.

Four weeks out - Organise how to move your home

We have shifted ourselves many times during our marriage, and it wasn't until we forked out the cost of a removalist that we realised that we would never do it ourselves again. If you are concerned about shifting yourself, at the very least, buy the correct tie-downs and restraint gear to ensure you minimise the damage to your belongings or hire a self-drive truck.

If you opt to pay a removalist to do the job, then there are a few pointers to keep in mind when choosing the right people. Ensure you ring around and get three quotes as they can vary as much as 30% in our experience. It isn't just about the price, though. It is a good idea to determine their reputation by reading Google reviews or other testimonials or asking friends and family who they used and if they were happy with the service provided. If you have large, unusual objects such as large safes and pianos, they will likely come out to conduct a more appropriate quote so that there are no surprises. Remember that it isn't unusual to request a copy of their insurance; after all, you trust them with your worldly possessions.

Two weeks out - Start packing!

It should take you two weeks to pack up your home, but you can also do it much quicker. When I was in the military, we could pack our house in two days, ready for a move at short notice! The more prepared and packed you are, the less the removalist will cost. You can buy packing boxes, paper, tape and bubble wrap at most of your storage and removal providers. Ensure you pack by room and don't mix up the boxes; they are cheap enough to have an extra one and write on them where they belong. Pack your non-essential items first, as two weeks is a long time to go without your coffee maker and toothbrush. Do not mark a box with the words "Valuables" or "Jewellery". I have even seen someone write "Cash Box" on one box, which is a quick way to let it go missing.

One week to go - The final countdown –

By this stage, you really should have the kitchen, bathroom and bedroom necessities left to pack. It is time to pack up your clothes, bedding, kitchen and bathroom, ready to put in the car and drive away. Make sure you do multiple final sweeps of the house to ensure you haven't left anything behind.

Chapter 16
Pre-settlement Inspection

Typically, during the week before the settlement of your new property, you are allowed to attend and conduct a pre-settlement inspection. So, what is a pre-settlement inspection? It is a chance for you to attend the property to ensure that the seller has met any specific conditions you may have negotiated into the sale contract. It is also a chance to ensure that the property is in a similar condition to when you inspected it initially and signed the contract of sale.

Usually, there is a period between when you first saw the property and settlement day, and anything could have happened. The property may have had tenants that didn't want to leave and kicked holes in the walls and ripped out windows and carpets. You, the buyer, have a right to inspect the property before settlement to ensure that the property is in the same condition and hasn't sustained any damage.

When you initially inspected the property and had a building and pest inspection conducted, you were looking for broken things that you could have the seller repair or replace. If items are broken or need replacing, you may have negotiated the replacement in the special conditions of the contract. The pre-settlement inspection is your last chance to look at the home before it settles into your name. It is an excellent chance to check that the property has no leftover rubbish and has been kept in a satisfactory condition since signing the contract of sale.

Try to conduct your pre-settlement inspection about a week from settlement to allow sufficient time for the seller to rectify any issues that may have become known. It would help if you organised to have your real estate agent with you when you inspect the property, as they have been involved with many transactions and generally know where to look.

What should you be looking for?

Significant damage

Whilst conducting your inspection, you're looking for any damage since you signed the contract. For example, you may notice a broken door; you should note this and then request it be fixed before settlement. If there is anything you are not sure about, ask questions.

Inclusions and exclusions

After you have negotiated inclusions and exclusions, ensure you go through them and that the inclusions are there and the seller has removed the exclusions. Inclusions may be furniture, blinds and dishwashers, and you want these to stay. Exclusions may also include rubbish or items that would cost you if they were to remain. Once again, take the contract of sale with you so you have the list to review and check off.

Condition

Most sellers will clean the property before handing it over to you. However, this isn't a requirement as they only have to hand the property over in a similar condition to how you inspected it. Buying and selling aren't like a rental agreement where they must "Bond Clean" the property before handing keys over. However, they remove all rubbish, and the property is presentable before settlement.

Special conditions

I mentioned previously about special conditions in the contract. Now is your chance to ensure the sellers meet the special conditions, like repairs to the property or resolving any matters affecting the property.

If you are unhappy with the property after the pre-settlement inspection, you need to notify your conveyancer and agent immediately. Your conveyancer and agent will then return to the seller's conveyancer to negotiate these terms to be met, or another agreement will be made.

Chapter 17
Settlement Day

Settlement day has finally come, and you are excited to get your keys to your new home. Well, hold up a little. There are a few things that have to happen today before you can get your keys. Settlement day is when the title for the property is officially and legally transferred into your name and this doesn't happen seamlessly. These days most settlements are made electronically, and once the conveyancers are satisfied that all legal requirements have been met, they press the "go" button. Once they push the "go" button, this is what happens in a nutshell:

- The buyer goes into more debt (if the money has been borrowed to buy the property).
- The seller gets out of debt a little.
- Agents and conveyancers get paid.
- The property is transferred into your name.

Once you have received confirmation from your conveyancer, give the selling agent a call before heading to their office to collect the keys. The selling agent needs to hear from the seller's conveyancer before releasing the keys to you, the buyer. Today, you are all that matters, and the settlement of this property is all you think. However, the seller's solicitor may have multiple settlements, which means they may not have recommended that the selling agent release the keys.

Congratulations! You have now successfully bought a property, picked up the keys, made it social media official, and started celebrating! Warning: don't celebrate too hard because you have to get up tomorrow morning to go to work and pay for your new home!

www.ingramcontent.com/pod-product-compliance
Lightning Source LLC
Chambersburg PA
CBHW020448220526
45464CB00002B/909